LIFE is
Good

A Book *of* Poetry

FARIN POWELL

authorHOUSE®

AuthorHouse™
1663 Liberty Drive
Bloomington, IN 47403
www.authorhouse.com
Phone: 1 (800) 839–8640

Published by AuthorHouse 12/23/2019

ISBN: 978-1-7283-3938-2 (sc)
ISBN: 978-1-7283-3939-9 (hc)
ISBN: 978-1-7283-3940-5 (e)

Library of Congress Control Number: 2019920606

Print information available on the last page.

For
Richard, Joanne, Brandy, Lenox, Bobby and Jimmy

Contents

Grief

Life Goes On

No Place to Go

Lives of Others

Grief

The Silent Enemy

The silent enemy doesn't declare war,
it only makes a phone call.
You don't see its enormous army,
you don't see its weapons,
you don't hear a single shot,
you hear its voice on the phone
and feel its fingers around your throat.
Then, suddenly, millions of creatures
move quietly under your skin,
attacking you
in your knees,
in your heart,
and in your brain.
Yes, the silent enemy never declares war,
it only makes a phone call.

I Tell Him Stories

I cringe every time
they stick the needle in his arm,
to find the *good* vein.
I ask him to look out the window,
the green garden has a good view.

I hold his free hand
as the poison drips into his vein.
I tell him funny stories,
he gives me his half smile.
Then, he closes his eyes
and listens.
I repeat the old stories
he has forgotten.
Some make him open his eyes,
some bring back the half smile.

The nurse checks the dripping bag,
the poison is in his blood now.
I thank her for a successful session,
then, I take him home
until the next chemo.

I Don't Want Your Heaven

Time after time, I repaired my nest
ruined by life's unexpected storms.
Time after time, I rode a train
escaping the ravaged memories.
Time after time, I said good-byes
to loved ones,
lying on hospital beds.
Then, I visited them,
in cemeteries
on different soils.

When the tumor chewed away
his words,
and stole his memory, bit by bit,
I was told,
"He has six months to live."
You're not God.
When he survived, friends told me
I'd go to Heaven, because
I had loved, suffered, and sacrificed.
I turned toward the sky and prayed,
"If reaching you brings this much pain,
I don't want your Heaven."

I Won't Cry

He's ready for an angel
to take him away.
I'm listening
to our favorite song;
his eyes are closed,
but his smile tells me
he's listening too.
I look around;
I see a man
fading away,
ready to depart.
It's New Year's Eve,
I have promised myself,
I won't cry.
The song reminds me
of our normal life;
when he used to
fix dinner,
bring me flowers
for no special occasion.
When he let
every one know
I was his queen.
The song has ended,
he's asleep now.
It's New Years Eve,
but the cave is getting darker.
I've promised myself
I won't cry.

Where Are You?

Everyday chores feel like
climbing a mountain,
finishing work in a hurry
I rush back home
give him medications.
Whether I'm cooking, or washing dishes,
I can hear him:
"Where are you?"
I rush back to his room;
his wounds are bleeding,
he keeps falling down.
I take him to the nearest ER,
and he's admitted.
The tumor is back,
He needs more tests;
The doctor sends me home.
I look at his empty bed, and
feel lonely.
Reaching for the phone,
I see a message waiting:
"Where are you?"
his voice sounds tired.

The next morning,
I buy some flowers,
and rush back to the hospital.
His bed is empty,
The nurse drops the phone
when she sees me,
"I was just calling you…
I'm so sorry…"

Every day,
I visit him, and
Lay flowers
on his grave.
I blow him a kiss,
and go home
to listen to his voice:
"Where are you?"

Life Is Good

Anytime he complained
about his chemo session, I said,
"Hey, no one's in hospital,
no one's dying. Life is Good."
For years I was
the cook, the driver, the nurse,
the cheerleader marching on
keeping him happy.
Like an army sergeant
I had to get my wounded soldier
out of the enemy zone.
I was the boxer
in the ring,
who got hit from every direction,
like a punching bag.
When the referee blew the whistle,
the fight stopped,
and I collapsed.

As I walked towards
the cemetery's gate;
the sad melody of a
cemetery scene in a movie
kept playing in my head.
I wish some memories
would die,
like animals, like humans,
like some plants.
but they don't,
they live forever.
Then they hunt you;

without any warning
in unexpected places,
at desperate times.
I was fighting my tears,
but felt better when the sky
began crying.
At the cemetery gate,
I thought I heard his voice:
"No one's in hospital,
no one *else* is dying,
"Life is Good."

How To Be Happy

Perhaps my mother taught me
how to take baby-steps,
and how to talk.
My father taught me
how to read newspapers.
My uncle read me books,
and took me to the movies.
A special teacher gave me
the courage to write
poems, to tell stories.
I discovered the gods of literature
on my own.
But no one taught me
how to be happy.
Then, one day
my prince charming showed up,
and took me to another land.
He taught me
how to throw out sadness-
like an old blanket,
how to build up
moments of joy
day after day.
He took my hand
and never let go.
When our happy days
turned into happy years,
an angel in Heaven got jealous
and took him away.

I remembered the old movie:
"Love is a Many Splendored Thing."
I learned from the movie
about the Chinese farmers;
when they feared
the angry and jealous gods,
they turned to the sky and yelled:
"Bad rice, bad rice."
When we were sailing
on the calm waves of the ocean
saying "Hello" to the daisies,
dancing the nights away,
laughing for no reason,
I should have turned to the sky,
raised my arms, and yelled:
"Bad rice, bad rice."
Alas, I forgot.
He didn't live long enough
to teach me
how to greet people
with a fake smile,
to fill the void in my heart
and live a happy life.

He Must Feel Cold

I see him through the window,
then, the image fades away.
I wait for him to call,
but the telephone is silent.
He's not coming,
dinner is getting cold.

Days passed.
I believed
this was a short trip.
He would come back
as usual,
with gifts and flowers.

The snowflakes are
dancing in the air now.
I wonder,
he must feel cold.
I should take his blanket,
and cover his grave.

The World Didn't Stop

When he died
the sun didn't stop shining,
the sky didn't cry,
the earth didn't shake.
Through the window,
I could see people
walking, chatting,
driving their cars.
Inside,
the nurses kept moving.
The world didn't stop
because he died.

I know when he died,
someone, somewhere said, "I do",
and then, kissed his bride.
Someone became grandpa
for the first time.
Someone had a party
celebrating his birthday,
a college degree or a new job.
The world didn't stop,
the parties went on.
no one cared that he died,
they didn't know him.

He died and
something died
in me.
Did I die too?
So, why am I worried?
he won't be here,
for my birthday,
for Valentine's Day
our anniversary,
the upcoming Christmas.
Oh, I forgot,
his memories…

I forgot memories never die.
They strike you,
like a thunderstorm
on a hot summer day.
They follow you,
like your shadow on the wall.
They appear on
your T.V. screen,
on your pillow, in your car,
and in every corner
of your house.
So, he didn't die.

It's Finally Over

I sit in my tepee made of three sticks,
and wait for the comet's arrival.
It has hit me before,
three times.
I see the blinding light,
I hear the deafening sound,
and I look at the sky.
A star is crying for me,
but the whole galaxy
is preparing for my funeral.
I see the light again,
I close my eyes,
I hear an explosion,
and I feel I'm falling down.
It's finally over.

How Dare You?

Don't you remember
how many times
I sat next to a pile of dirt
and said "goodbye" to a loved one?
Don't you remember
how many times
I hit a stone wall
and had to start all over again?
Don't you remember
all the challenges
I faced in life,
and all the sad moment endured?
Don't you remember
you promised me
"happily ever after"?
So, how dare you
leave me in this jungle
called life?
How dare you leave me
with stacks of medical bills,
your long list of debts
and a bleeding heart.

And now, how dare you
come to my dream, smiling,
as if nothing has changed?
How dare you
tell me I can still fly
on the wings of the wind
and have breakfast with the sun?
Tell me,

what I'm supposed to do with
my unfinished poems,
your dying garden, and
your ghost following me
all day long?

After a few minutes of
silent crying,
she felt some serenity.
She arranged the flowers
on his grave,
blew him a kiss and whispered:
"See you tomorrow."

I Have No Desire To Leave

I climbed the mountain
a million times
ran through the fire
felt I died.
Now that race is over;
no more chemo sessions,
no more MRIs
no more pounding heart
to hear the doctor's prediction,
no more fire under my skin,
It's just me and
his lonely grave.
He invites me to join him
but I won't.

I've no desire to leave.
I see the younger me; she has
so many songs to sing,
so much laughter to give,
and so many stories to tell.
The younger me
wants to forget the sadness,
say "Hello" to the sun, and
dance in the meadows.
The younger me is alive
excited about the unknown,
She still wonders
what's waiting for her
at the end of the road.
She wants to take the journey,
and I won't stop her.

Life Goes On

God Listens

God listens to his creatures
wherever they choose to reach him.
The butterfly sits
on the most colorful flower.
The bird finds the tallest tree,
the lion climbs on the highest hill,
and the gazelle runs
through the greenest meadow.
I walk to the ocean
to feel his presence,
to talk to him.
I see the magnitude of his splendor,
my words fade away
like the foam of the ocean wave.

I Want To Scream

I want to scream, a scream that reaches
as high as the sky, a scream
as strong as the voice of a preacher,
as noble as the prophecy of a prophet.

I want to resist
like an angry warrior,
like a brave hero,
like a strong solid dam.

I want to imprison
all crook politicians,
along with my neighbor
who believes life is a Disney Land.

I want to be soft
like a velvety blue sky,
like a morning mist,
like a silk night gown.

I want to sail
to the shore,
to the dawn,
to the last horizon.

I want to search for the loved one I lost;
until the end of the road,
until the last gaze,
until the last word.

I want to have mercy
like the kind heart of a mother.
Like rain washing the dirt,
I want to wash away everyone's pain.

I want to scream, a scream that reaches
as high as the sky, a scream
as strong as the voice of a preacher,
as noble as the prophecy of a prophet.

I Used To See Rainbows

I used to say hello
to my daffodils in the garden.
I had my kite ready to fly
even on rainy days.
I used to see rainbows
painting the sunny sky.
I used to enjoy walking
the winding roads.
I used to love life.
What happened
that I stopped
seeing, hearing, and feeling?
Now, I miss
being hungry,
being excited.
I miss feeling alive.

No Life And No Pain

Yesterday, I asked God,
"Am I being tortured
for my past sins?"
have I committed a crime?"
I didn't get any answer,
then, I begged Him
to punish me
when I am on the other side,
I asked him,
to throw me in his hell fire,
& to scatter my ashes over the mountains.
I bargained a good deal;
on the other side, there is
no office to go to,
no waiting in the lines,
no cooking, cleaning, driving,
no financial worries,
no kids to worry about,
no sleepless nights
caring for a sick loved one,
no doctors appointments,
no chemo sessions,
no life and no pain.

Broken Heart

"You've broken heart syndrome,"
the doctor says.
What a poetic title
for a sickness that can't be cured!
Little veins break,
around your heart, you don't see the blood,
but you feel the burning.
The cells die, and then,
they revive when you breathe.

Years ago, her son left home,
without a word,
leaving her with a broken heart.
She's traveling on a train,
but the images travel with her,
the scary nights
when his fever reached the roof,
the first day of school,
his prom night, his college years.

She gets off the train & goes home;
some one has painted his face
on the pane of the windows,
on the wall,
on her pillow.
She puts her hand on her chest,
feels the heartbeat and wonder:
how much more broken can it get?
Why don't you let go?

She looks at the closed door of his room,
She can still hear his voice.
She misses his laughter,
his jokes…
The dreams she had for him,
die one by one.
She won't be seeing his wedding,
She won't be watching his child grow,
instead, she'll be asking *why* forever.

Don't Erase My memories

I tell my hands,
don't give me aches and pain,
I still have to write.

I tell my brain,
don't erase my memories,
they keep me alive.

I tell my eyes,
don't blur the images,
I expect to see new faces & places.

I tell my heart,
don't quit on me,
I need to finish this journey.

The Bird Returns

I tell my friends:
"If you ever saw me happy,
don't be jealous."
I was not destined to be happy."
The happiness I know is like a bird
that finds me sometimes
in odd places, or
unexpected times.
It sits on my roof,
for a little while.
Then, it gets bored,
and flies away.
The bird doesn't see the destruction
it leaves behind.
and never knows about my pain.

Years later,
when I've got all
the broken pieces
glued together,
and overcome the pain,
the bird returns;
singing again,
giving me hope,
this time, he'll stay.
But he flies away,
leaving me wondering
how long I should wait;
another year,
another decade,
or maybe forever.

The Alley

The alley near our house
seems like a piece of Heaven
thrown on earth.
The tall trees on both sides
make green walls,
nesting the sparrows.
The changing colors in the fall
cannot be copied
by Monet or Van Gogh.
Alas, like any good thing in life
the alley is short;
it connects to the highway
and disappears,
like a river
pouring to the ocean.

You Bring Your Chandeliers

When the wind attacks the trees
the clouds cry
and the rain slaps the windows
you call me on the phone,
and talk to me till my fear disappears.

When my skin starts burning
and every cell in my body
dies of thirst,
you bring me the river
to kill the fire.

When the stars lose their diamonds,
the sky turns black
and I feel like a prisoner
you carve a window,
and invite the sun.

When anxiety attacks
targeting my heart
and leaves holes
like the bullets of a machine gun
you build me a fortress.

When the sparrows stop singing
The daisies die in my garden
and I'm searching to find
the lost words
you listen.

When I stop dreaming,
sitting in my tepee
waiting for the next melancholia
and my room gets darker,
you bring your chandeliers.

Have You Ever Wondered?

The good book says,
on Judgment Day,
God will destroy the mountains and
turn them into ashes.
But, have you ever wondered
what he does on a normal day?
Does he lift up a curtain to watch
the earth from time to time?
Does he control every thing
from a computer room?
or rule the world by pointing
his fingers to different directions?
Does he have a favorite language
to speak or to hear?
Does he sleep at night,
or drink coffee in the morning?
Does he ever watch hurricanes,
earthquakes, or tsunamis?
or ask his angels to report on
famine, poverty or wars?
In his Heaven,
does he allow people to built
churches, synagogues, or mosques?
Does he ever get sad, or shed a tear
watching a tragedy?
Does he ever pause?
a last minute doubt:
who lives, who dies?

Does he ever see me
walking on a shaky ground,
waiting for the next tragedy?
Does he ever hear my silent cry?

Broken Wings

No border to stop them,
no passport or visa required,
no airline tickets,
no airport security check,
no immigration clearance,
birds are free to fly.
They speak the same language,
and sing similar songs.
They're not scared of
earthquakes, tornados, or hurricanes,
They escape bombs and missiles,
Yet each can easily get killed
by a man's bullet,
or placed in a cage.

I know a bird in a cage.
There are burns
on her wounded wings;
she can't fly.
But she dreams of flying
over the meadows,
in the vast blue sky
reaching the sun.
The divorce judge
opened the cage,
showed her the road to freedom.
yet, she still felt confined
in a larger cage,
with an open door.

No more captivity,
but the broken wings
wouldn't heal,
she couldn't fly.

The Ultimate Art

My mentor told me:
"Painting is the ultimate art";
doesn't need words to describe it,
or a language to draw it.
I agreed; I was sixteen.
Hundreds of poems later,
and thousands of words
dancing on pages of my novels,
I still believed in *the ultimate art*,
envied the painters,
until the pain began.
Searching for a lost soul,
never finding an answer,
never learning why,
I needed the words
words to replace the tears
words to heal the wounds.
I wrote to my mentor:
"You can't paint the pain."

Acting Like God

My sister told me,
you write stories,
choosing which character
hits the wall
for every step it takes.
Which character
has an easy life,
who lives,
who dies.
When telling a story,
you're acting like God.
But some one else
is writing your book,
telling future stories
you don't know.
She is right;
so, I'll be waiting
curious to know
how the Almighty
writes my story,
how he'll end
the last chapter.

Would Someone Please Get Married

I remember the days
that I danced
at my friends weddings;
they danced at mine.
Then, I saw friends' children
getting married.
Nowdays I only see weddings
on my TV or at the movies.
I feel like sticking my head
through the window
and shout:
"Would some one please get married."

Tunnel of Lights

On a beautiful sunny day,
little white clouds kept running
like playful kids.
The clouds formed a tunnel,
I was pulled into the tunnel of lights,
flying over mountains and oceans.
A force dropped me on a land,
I saw a garden full of roses stretched to eternity.
An intoxicating scent made me feel dizzy.
A hand pushed me to a gate and whispered:
"This is the first heaven."
I saw beautiful torches of fire,
and prophet Zoroaster lecturing students,
I bowed and said a prayer.
The wind took me to the second heaven,
I saw prophet Muhammad giving some booklets
to a group of feminists,
I bowed and said a prayer.
The clouds formed another tunnel
and the wind took me to the third heaven.
I saw Jesus talking to a group of demonstrators
carrying signs which read: "Gay rights,"
I bowed and said a prayer.
The wind took me to the fourth heaven,
I saw Moses mediating two groups of angry people,
I bowed and said a prayer.
The clouds formed another tunnel of lights,
and the wind pushed me through
and put me behind the gate of the seventh heaven.
I saw Abraham with three books on his lap,

I got closer to ask him a question.
He pointed to a garden behind him and said:
"Only the Creator can answer that question."
I bowed and said a prayer.

......

The dream is over,
I am awake now believing
one day He'll tell the world,
why we have different religions.

No Place to Go

Every Now And Then

Every now and then
life stops moving
on the right path.
Some one else makes decisions
and your happy life
gets interrupted.

Every now and then
your joyful days are over;
and your plans fall apart.
You can't travel,
see a movie,
or even visit a friend

Every now and then
your doctor's office
resembles an interrogation room,
you feel like a victim
ready to be questioned
by the cops.

Every now and then
Your room gets darker,
the walls around you
move closer
and you feel
you're in prison.

Every now and then
you end up serving tea
to people who come
to extend their condolences.
Their sympathies resemble
dying bouquets of flowers.

Every now and then
the warden opens
the prison door,
but outside the gate
no one's waiting,
you've no place to go.

The Last Walk Alone

He was dying,
he didn't want my mother to know.
He traveled thousands of miles
to die in my town.
He explained his trip:
"I hadn't seen you for too long."
He had chosen me to witness
his last journey.
We walked to the pond every day,
he fed the ducks,
We read the papers together,
listened to music,
I never knew my father was dying.
A phone call from ER to my office,
he was gone before I reached the hospital.
He didn't give me a chance to pray,
to bargain with God,
to delay his journey.
He didn't let me say "Goodbye,"
he walked the last walk alone.
His mission accomplished;
he saved my mother the agony;
created an image that
he was still traveling.
He had left a suitcase by his bed,
full of gifts, each wrapped
in a box with a name tag;
that was his way of saying "goodbye."
My gift, an antique gold coin,
and a thick spiral notebook,
autographed inside:
"to my princess,
write the story."

In My Dreams

In my dreams,
I'm sitting by the river,
watching a piece of wood
hitting the rocks, drifting
with no control over its destiny.
In my dreams,
I'm walking on an unknown road,
and the monster keeps following me.
I'm drowning in an ocean,
and he's laughing at the shore.
In my dream
I'm running aimlessly in a forest,
and I see the monster
hiding behind the trees.
Finally, I find a cave
and the monster disappears;
I am in my last resting place.

That Sick Pansy In The Garden

You live once,
you die once.
I heard that somewhere,
don't remember who said it?
I saw my mother,
sitting on the edge of my bed,
the bed moved when she stood up.
But, she had died years ago.
Was I dreaming? Was I awake?
I would never know.

I chose this house,
with its fancy decoration,
cheerful garden full of my
favorite flowers;
I once loved this house.
I don't feel it's mine anymore,
maybe because of
all the shouting outside,
all the silence inside,
or my empty heart.

I write poems
when I feel like screaming.
I write a novel
When I feel bored.
The singer's song fills the room,
the lyrics keep repeating
in my head,

all day,
long after
the song has ended.

You die once,
Why did he die
for five years
day after day?
Why do I feel like
that sick pansy in the garden?
I die every night,
and revive every morning.
when the sun
smiles at me.

When the death angel
Pulls my hand,
I won't scream,
I won't cry,
because no one sees me
no one hears me.
I only keep calling God,
no response.
I wait for a sign,
then I give up.

I Don't Have Enough Tears

I have enough tears to cry for
all battered women in the world,
all neglected children left behind,
all poverty stricken lands in Africa,
all rape victims punished for their rapists' crimes,
all the sad words carved on graves,
all the fallen towers,
and all the soldiers killed in unjust wars.

But I don't have enough tears to cry for
your broken promises,
your poisonous words,
the stormy journey you took me on,
the sinking boat you forced me to sail,
the long scary nights,
and my lonely wedding band
sitting on the dresser.

The Same Road

You paint the beauty,
better than any painter.
Like a sculptor, you can mold
a woman's body in your head.
Ignoring reality, you choose
your praising words carefully.
Like a pond of water,
you are full of deceits.
I know
the crow is a poor bird,
the cactus is a lonely plant,
and the creek next to our house
moans like an injured man.
I also know
I have repeated the same mistakes,
have walked the same road, and
have endured the same pain.
But this time you and my pain
have to leave my heart
and find another home.

You Had No Right

You had no right to come
to my dream last night.
You had no right to bring me
flowers and your apology.
You had no right to wear
your dazzling smile,
and ignite a dying love.
You had no right to build up
my dream house and invite me in.
You had no right to sit
on the deck, wipe my tears
& make me laugh.
And you had no right
to disappear and end my dream.

Year After Year

You didn't buy him a gift
for his birthday, or Christmas.
You didn't read him a book
at bed time.
You didn't take him to a game,
or teach him to ride a bike.
You didn't take him to school,
or attended his sport activities.
Years later, you didn't know
where his college was,
you didn't celebrate
his graduation.
Yet, year after year, I reminded him'
"Don't forget The Father's Day."

Fate IS A Lonely Writer

I sit by the nearby creek,
bur I don't hear
the soothing sound of the water.
I pick flowers in my garden
but I don't enjoy the aroma.
It's sad to walk
on the same path
and repeat the same journey
day after day.
Words attack my brain,
but the page in front of me is blank.
I have a title for my next novel:
"Fate is a lonely writer."
Now I need to fill
the blank pages
one day at a time.

The Bus is Running Fast

The bus is running fast;
from the bus's window
I can see the street,
men, women.
The bus is running faster,
now everyone seems to be
running faster.
The bus slows down;
I see more men and women.
Maybe I should get out
follow them on the street,
and ask a burning question.
"would you exchange
your life with me?"
I'm ready to gamble;
selling my life,
living some one else's.

You and I

You and I have traveled
on two trains, running parallel,
close enough to witness
our stories unfold,
yet too far away to say "Hello."

I watched you playing
with your little girl,
then, facing a painful divorce,
and ultimately when you found
your everlasting love.

You watched me playing
with my little girl,
then my nasty divorce
and ultimately when I found
my everlasting love.

When the melancholia
shattered my planet,
you got off your train
and rode in mine
holding my hands.

The crisis is over now,
we are back on our trains,
still running parallel.
But now, I can wave and mouth the words,
thank you my friend.

Someone Will Rise

With the dreaded sound of the wind,
with every jolt of a curtain,
with the striking sound of a thunder,
for years, I have been waiting
for someone to come, someone to rise.
I want him to inject a pure fetus into the soil.
I know the fetus will grow into many plants,
the plants will bloom, and every blossom
will spread the message of hope.
With a wet woolen rag, my Hero
would wipe all tarnished hearts,
all resentful rusty feelings.
So, at the time of war,
everyone will hug.
And during a depression everyone
will share their good fortune.

I know that my fearful heart,
reflects the world's restlessness.
I know that one day, someone will rise.
He'll dust the dirt off his body,
and leave the yawning land
and the yawning years behind.
Angry with the callousness of the earth,
my Hero will kick every speck of soil.
He will give an anti-sleeping pill
to every soul, plowing their thoughts.
Like a messiah, he will gaze directly
into the eyes of the sky,

and demand an earthquake to shake everyone up.
With the striking sound of a thunder,
I have been waiting
for someone to come, some one to rise.

The Bird Doesn't Know About The War

The snowy days are long gone,
and the spring is finally here.
I see the white blossoms outside my window,
but covered with blood.
My window is ready to steal
the first fresh spring air.
I turn the pages of my newspaper hurriedly,
avoiding the pictures of:
wounded children, fallen soldiers.
I feel someone's hands squeezing my throat,
oh, I can't breathe.
A happy bird is flying by,
but I feel like crying.
I remember a favorite poem:
"The bird does not read the newspaper,"
and I say to myself:
"The bird doesn't know about the war."
I listen to the song on the radio,
"What a Wonderful World,"
I close my eyes and remember
another song, "What's going on…?"

Lives of Others

My Neighbor

My neighbor
at the end of the alley
celebrates Christmas
in October,
long before Halloween.
She leaves the decoration
until the month of March.
I wonder why she needs
six months of celebration!
Is she happy
during the rest of the year?
No one knows;
she doesn't talk to anyone,
she walks her dog
late at night
when the alley is asleep.

Chaos At The Terminal

She had a nagging headache,
and a bit of jetlag.
Her guilt felt heavier
than her suitcase.
Those boring conferences
kept her away from
her little girl.
It was a part of her job.
Single mom, raising a five-year old,
she needed the money.
She called her daughter.
"Grandma, Mommy's home,"
her angel screamed over the phone.
A twenty minute taxi ride
would take her home.
She imagined hugging her daughter,
showering her with surprise gifts.
The noise around her
disrupted her thoughts,
there was chaos at the terminal.
A huge number of people
standing there, some shouting,
some carrying signs.
She asked a protestor,
"What's going on?"
"People from some Muslim countries
can't come here anymore,"
he replied.
She saw many sad faces;
some people crying,
a woman pleading
with the security officer:

"please release my father;
he's old, and has a heart condition."
She looked around,
and listened to the protesters
for a few minutes.
Then, she found an empty chair,
in a far corner of the terminal.
She sat there,
opened her briefcase,
tore up a page, and copied
the words of a sign
carried by a small group of people.
She then joined the group,
and held her paper high.
the sign read:
"Do you need a lawyer?"

Like A Grave

The chain felt heavier
around her neck;
she ignored her ankle's bleeding
and kept walking.
She passed her son's school,
stopped at the park
he used to play.
She sat on a stone bench
and remembered
his laughter on the swing.

She stood up and kept walking.
she reached her old home;
the magnolia tree still covered
a big part of the house.
She located the windows
of her bedroom.
She remembered
her sad life
behind those windows.

She passed the courthouse,
remembered
the custody hearing and
how she lost her little boy.
She looked up to the sky,
hoping for an angel's help,
the sun hid behind the cloud.
She reached the lake,
no one was around,

no boat sailing,
not even a single duck.
The lake looked lonelier than
her heart.

She passed the church,
stood by the closed door,
remembered her father's funeral,
and the joyful cheers
on her wedding.
She kept walking
the road was blocked.
She turned around
walked home, and
crawled into her bed.
The bed felt like a grave.

A Beautiful Mind

His kind eyes
and inviting smile
welcomed everyone
to his home.
He wasn't famous, but
had many admirers.
He wasn't rich, but
had a treasure in his brain,
a beautiful mind.
When a stroke rocked his boat,
it interrupted his life,
but couldn't steal his treasure–
the beautiful mind.

He was moved to a
strange place, a foreign land.
He didn't complain,
he didn't mind.
He remembered the faces
of his visitors,
but wondered about their names.
His fragile body slowed him down
but the beautiful mind kept moving.
The images on TV helped him
create characters,
and tell their stories,
to different people,
to any one who listened.

The day he traveled to
the other side,
although expected,
he left behind
many broken hearts,
many tearful eyes.
They came from near and far,
to celebrate his life,
to say goodbye
to a beautiful mind.

For Myisha

The Silent Sister

She was ten
when her mother disappeared.
Exiting the school bus in a hurry
she was excited
to show her
an all "A" report card,
but Mom wasn't home.
She found her sister crying,
and her two aunts arguing.

She didn't understand
why everyone was fighting
to get custody of her,
why the judge gave
her sister to a foster family.
"She's only twelve."
the aunts cried out.
"You two are not fit,"
the judge said.
She wiped her tears,
but felt happy
when "grandma"
took her home.
She had her own room,
life was peaceful,
but she missed her mom.
She kept dreaming
one day mom would show up
at home,
or the school;
that never happened.

Years went by,
she finished college
still dreaming to find
the missing mom.
Every time she passed
through the old neighborhood,
she wondered;
was her mom there?
was she held captive?
or being tortured?
was she buried alive?
When the police closed the case
of a missing woman,
her sister became a cop
to find their mother,
but she didn't live long enough,
another tragedy,
she died.
The younger sister
had to witness her funeral.
The mourners cried,
but the silent sister
only screamed inside.
Her two aunts kept repeating:
"Who dies in her 20's?
of lung cancer?"
"She never smoked!"

The silent sister climbed
the ladder of success,
post graduate degree,
a fascinating job,
yet, she carried

a hole in her heart.
Until one day…
she met her soul mate.
She looked like a princess
in her satin wedding gown,
yet she felt
like an orphan.
The new love
took her to a different world
full of joy and happiness,
but it couldn't heal
the old wound.
It was still bleeding
every now and then,
when the memories
would hit her
at different times,
or different places.
Days went by, and
one day…
the family doctor told her,
"You feel nauseous
because you're pregnant.
Months later,
in a hospital
when the nurse put
her baby in her arms—
a daughter…she sighed.
She touched the baby's face,
the old wound had healed,
and the pain was gone.
She kissed the baby's face
wiped her tears,
and looked at the sky.
Thank you Mom.

The Old Man

He yanks a few weeds,
before he picks up
his morning papers.
In the afternoon, he rakes
the leaves in his front yard,
all seven of them.
When he waits for the mailman,
I pray he gets some good news
To make him happy.
But he never smiles,
or opens his door
allowing me to say "Hello."
The neighbor across the street
has warned me,
"The old man never accepts help.
Haven't you seen his sign?
'No trespassing'."
He has no visitor,
except occasional paramedics
taking him away in the ambulance.
When he's gone, I pray for him
to return soon, to do
his daily chores.

Yesterday, I saw a young woman
hugging him.
"She must be his daughter," I thought.
Then, I saw her erecting the sign,
"For Sale."

I'll miss the old man,
although relieved.
I won't hear the siren of another ambulance,
I won't see his last trip to the hospital
and I won't know if he's gone forever.

Every Night

There is no one around
no good news,
except absurdity
dancing in her room.
Every night,
she opens the window, and
feels the breeze caressing her hair.
Her eyes follow
the shining stars in the sky.
She listens to the sound of footsteps,
fading away in the alley.
The alley goes to sleep,
like a dead being, but
she stays awake.
Pressing her face on her pillow.
she longs to see his face,
one more time.
He'll return home some day.

The Mourning Dove

Through the thick branches
of the magnolia tree,
the mourning dove still watches her.
But the woman with a suitcase
ignores the bird.
Her life is shattered,
another death, another funeral,
another cemetery.
She hears the bird singing,
but has no intention to look outside.
She remembers the bird,
how it used to follow her
from one continent to another,
one city to another.
The bird brought her happiness,
or she thought it did.
The bird is a sign
telling her to leave town,
to find happiness
some where else.
But the woman with a suitcase
has no desire to leave;
there's no one out there
waiting for her.

What A Journey

She was happy with her "no life" existence,
in a basement full of books, papers and boxes.
She climbed mountains to finish a normal day,
running in all directions, raising kids.
On a stormy day in her life,
while holding on to a branch,
struggling to survive, a firm hand pulled
her away from the cliff; she was saved.
"Can you use some help?" the kind voice asked.
"No", she gave him a cold look.
The stranger ignored the response,
and took her for a walk.
They talked, shared life stories,
they paused, they laughed.
Before they knew it,
they were in Heaven.
They danced to their favorite songs,
in God's backyard, they reached euphoria
without breaking any man-made laws.
What a journey, what a year, what a life.

On another stormy day in her life,
the clouds caved in and dropped her
back to the earth, washing her away
like a little pebble.
She is back in her basement existence again,
buried in books, papers and boxes.
Running in all directions,
she is learning to survive the next storm;
but this time,
she owns a piece of Heaven.

The Yellow Cab

She gives her son a hug
he picks up his suitcase,
the yellow cab enters the driveway.
He gets into the cab
waves at her with a lovely smile.
She blows a kiss,
the cab heads for the airport.

Years ago,
at a hospital in a foreign land,
she gave birth
to a baby boy.
When the baby's little fingers
grabbed hers tight,
an eternal love seed
was planted in her heart.
She remembered his joyful play
in the bathtub with his rubber duck,
his first words,
first clumsy steps, and
the crayon drawings on the wall.

Work days brought her pain;
every time she left him behind.
Years later, she felt the same pain
when she left him at his college dorm.
The cab has disappeared from her view now;
inside the house, no more the sound of his laughter
only sadness filling the air,
like an invisible smoke.
She wipes her tears;
and starts counting the days

until the next college break,
or a big holiday.
She longs for the day that
the yellow cab appears again
in her driveway.

Did She Scare Him?

Talking to him was like
reading a poem to a ferocious ocean,
or singing a song for the wind.
He listened, but
he didn't intend to hear.
He's not coming tonight;
she opens the window
and invites the fresh air.
The wind dances
with the branches of
the tall trees.
The images are scary
under the moonlight.
She wonders:
did she scare him with
the gifts, her poems,
her love,
or her mere existence?

Searching For A Few Worms

Every night, in her dream,
in her prettiest evening gown,
standing tall and proud,
she keeps looking at her long red fingernails.
She hears a voice:
"Why don't you give up?"
Every night, in her dream, in a quiet cemetery,
she sees someone digging in the dirt,
searching for a few worms to survive with.
She sees a shadow kneeling, digging more in the dirt.
She sees the blood dropping
from her long red fingernails,
she sees the worms, and feels like vomiting.
Then, she sees the shadow rising,
dusting off her long evening gown,
and moving away.
Every night, in her dream,
she sees bloody hands with long red fingernails
raised towards the sky,
and she hears a woman begging:
"Is there some one out there?"
There is no answer, except the wind.
Every night in her dream,
she sees a train passing by,
a train full of masquerading people.
she see the train speeding up,
and two hands with long red finger nails,
trying to catch the train.
She feels like screaming:
"Please take her with you."
No sound comes out of her mouth,
she feels something icy running down her spine,

then she hears the collapse of a body in a grave;
a beautiful body with a long evening gown.
she sees the dirt shoveled into the grave,
the body is almost covered now,
except two hands with long red fingernails.
she hears some one crying, someone praying,
she says to herself: "This must be the wind."

She had No Answer

How deep is your love?
The song was popular when they met.
A two-day conference
turned into
hurried happy moments,
and dreamlike days.
New York connected
with San Francisco,
the phone calls,
the trips,
they reached Heaven;
they were in love.
But his past life
surfaced like a killer hurricane
raging over a calm ocean.
Then, a revolution shook the earth
taking her thousands of miles away
and changed their destiny.
The two connected hearts
drifted apart.
How deep is your love?
When she heard the song again,
she had no answer.
To keep her sanity,
she began listening
to another song,
How can you mend a broken heart?

He Loves Sundays

Every place is closed on Sundays;
no mail delivering bad news,
no job interviews,
and no rejections,
so, he loves Sundays.
He arranges the piles of bills
on his desk,
he doesn't have the heart
to count the rejection letters.
He stares at two pictures
on his desk;
a happy boy with
a baseball bat,
a pretty wife
with a Doris Day smile.
He squeezes his brain,
he doesn't know how
he got there—no job!
It's half past midnight;
it's almost Monday,
the beginning of
a long week
and a journey to nowhere.

The Pain Doesn't Die

Like an uninvited guest,
the pain entered her life.
It is drinking her coffee,
chewing on her food,
and sleeping in her bed.
Like her grown shadow,
it walks with her,
whenever she tries to escape.
Like a mean neighbor,
it builds walls around her.
Like a brain tumor, it pushes her
closer to death, every moment;
the pain doesn't die.
Every morning, it sits in the mirror,
staring at her
ready to cut her heart,
and drown her in her blood.
Life is passing her by,
like an express train.
She wants to catch the train,
but the pain pulls her long skirt,
holding her back.
The pain follows her everywhere,
like a prison guard.
She smiles and says "Hello"
to people on the street,
they see her, but not the pain.
no one knows
she lost a loved one;
the pain doesn't die.

The Shadow On The Wall

Walking through the
playground of his childhood,
he remembered that no one ever read
a scary story to him;
he never had a monster dream.
But he knew that the shadow on the wall
was a monster ready to attack him.
He finished reading his book,
took some notes and closed his eyes,
but he could still see the monster.
For months, the monster had followed him,
sat in his classroom, occupied a desk
like the rest of his students.
The monster listened to his lecture every day
and followed him home every night.
The monster was quiet during the day,
but at night, it was shrill like a roaring ocean,
it was even more scary when it was silent.
He thought one day one of his students
would write on the blackboard:
"The professor lives with a monster,"
then the news of his secretive torment
would travel everywhere in town.
He looked at his depressed bed,
longed to go to sleep, but
the shadow was still on the wall;
he didn't want the monster in his bed,
so, he left his house.
He walked through the new park,
and tossed a pill to the air,
feeling better believing he had defeated
his doctor and the monster both.

He came back home, the shadow on the wall
was shaky and pale,
the monster was worn out now.
He closed his eyes and smiled.
He was planning
for the monster's funeral

The Fear Of A Lonely Woman

During her childhood
she was afraid of grandma's stories,
full of ghosts,
of nights and darkness, and
running footsteps in the alley.
She was scared of the clashes
of the tree branches with the wind, and
the lightning in the sky
which would turn the city naked in a second.
As she grew older she feared
earthquakes, floods, and wars.
Years later when he said he loved her,
she trembled like a scared bird,
She wondered if they would split,
what if they repeated
the fate of the other lovers!

After all those years, the woman is still fearful,
this time it is not the fear of grandma's stories,
or the fear of natural disasters or the wars.
This is the fear of a lonely woman,
who is sailing in the creek of no hope.
like a lily, the woman
cannot change her destiny.

His Journey Is Almost Over

He has met rich people with
no need to work, no brain to think,
yet ruling
like kings and queens.

He has cared for kids from broken homes,
who lost liberty behind bars,
struggling to break
the curse of their poverty.

He has seen sick love,
comfortable marriages,
nasty divorces, meaningless hugs,
and has heard fake "I love you."

He has witnessed superpowers
come and go, seen
cout d'etats, famines, wars
and destruction of little nations.

He has sensed
God's anger,
watching natural disasters
that made Biblical stories pale.

He has been surprised by
political leaders who sold
their souls for power,
and scared people, acting like God.

He has admired those who tried
to balance the scale of justice by
giving everyone
a wake-up pill.

Now, his journey is almost over;
he needs a blinder, a pill of stupidity, and
a pair of comfortable shoes
to walk to his retirement home.

Distant Refuge

Wearing a long white satin gown,
the woman dances in
the green hill of her imagination.
A symphony orchestra follows this ballerina
wherever she goes.
The sound of a violin describes her sad life,
the pounding on the piano keys
gives her energy to slide,
and the symbol reflects her rage.
The kind meadow is her distant refuge,
where the sound of music soothes her soul.
She sips on every raindrop coming her way,
she tiptoes after every tune is played.
She is full of passion and thirsty for love
The dance in the meadow gives her serenity,
and the voice inside keeps her going:
Don't lose your mind.

The Kingmaker

It was not just their numbers
he remembered,
he knew the man and the woman
behind every number.
He made his daily *list*,
not knowing he was paying
other people's bills, mortgages,
and college tuitions.
His open-door policy,
and his smiling face
invited everyone to his office.
He survived working with professionals
who argued all day long
making a living.
When the gods in black robes
descended and tied his hands,
he still kept making the *list*.
He still remembered
the man and the woman
behind every number.
Whether he's sipping
on his tropical *tiki* in Hawaii,
or watching a game,
he'll be missed forever,
as a friend, a brother, or the king-maker.

The Bridge Over The Pond

She sat by the pond, looking at the bridge,
her eyes searched for a house,
the home she lived in many years ago.
The house was still there
on the other side of the pond.
She remembered her little boy
and a strange angry man called husband,
a man who raped her soul
every day and night, over and over.
She remembered those depressing days,
self- imprisoned in her cold sullen room,
counting every moment until the next day.
During the dark nights,
she walked over the bridge,
in her silent clamor, she questioned God's godhood.
She cried and waited for a gleaming star,
she feared for her life and her son's,
but no one came to her rescue, no one cared.
She remembered some happy moments,
the return of her little boy from school every day,
his laughter when he fed the ducks,
and the angry man's departure.
She remembered the wrecked ship of her life,
the odd jobs, the long hours, and the piles of bills.
The woman wiped her tears, and watched the ducks.
A hand offered some bread and a voice said,
"Mom, today you feed the ducks."

Author's Bio

Farin Powell practices law in Washington D.C. In addition to many legal publications in European and American law journals and law reviews, Powell has published short stories and poems in various literary magazines and poetry anthologies. Her most recent poem was chosen for *Poets to Come*—an anthology celebrating Walt Whitman's Bicentennial Birthday. She has received many awards, including two from the D.C. Bar Association; a Special Merit Award in 2005, and a Distinguished Merit Award in 2010. For her pro bono work and her novels, she also received the Women of Impact Award from *Focus on Women Magazine* in 2016. *Life is Good* is her second book of poetry. Her first one titled *A Piece of Heaven* was published in 2010. Powell is also the author of four novels; *Two Weddings, Roxana's Revolution, The Judge,* and *The Mother. Roxana's Revolution* received the Editor's Choice Award and was chosen as book of the week by Bookworks.com. *The Judge* is a legal thriller which has received over 250 good reviews on Amazon.com and Amazon U.K., and 800 positive ratings on Goodreads.

www.farinpowell.com
www.farinpowellbooks.com
Amazon.com *The Judge*, Farin Powell page
Twitter account: @farinpowell